# "WHAT CAME FIRST THE EGG (REASON) OR THE HEN (EMOTIONS)?"

A BioPsychoSocial (BPS) Model
of Reality, an Update

DR. ANGELL O. DE LA SIERRA, ESQ.

*Trafford rev. 02/01/2019*

 www.trafford.com

**North America & international**
toll-free: 1 888 232 4444 (USA & Canada)
fax: 812 355 4082

# INTRODUCTION

## "WHAT CAME FIRST THE EGG (REASON) OR THE HEN (EMOTIONS)?"

Any time we deal with complex objects and/or phenomena it is proper to ask what, when or where is it happening or happened before we even think of why? Or do we first avoid its negative effects when present or perhaps get closer to experience its positive detectable consequences? Before we may continue further in the analysis of 'causality' one can ask, i.e, was the measured or observable object/event the cause or the consequence of that subjective experience? But what if the cause is beyond the sense-phenomenal resolution of the human observer, or the measurable/observable signs or symptoms take a longer time to be effectively recorded? Furthermore, any analysis will have to reckon with both the well-known cognoscitive sense-phenomenal and logical limitations of the relevant human narrative language (the only species historically recorded!). How can we attain an absolute truth about our reality, life and consciousness? Is such 'destination' goal an illusion or must we only consider it as a 'journey' through an ever-changing vital environment, an evolving destination? If so, Quo Vadis homo sapiens? Was Sigmund Freud's mysterious libido-controlled unconsciousness (See his Interpretation of Dreams.) in control of the hormone-determined subjective emotional state or was the latter causally efficient to initiate/precede the effective behavioral adaptive survival of the human species or just its consequence? Or maybe we will never know 'why' and thus incorporate the 'theosophical' driving force argument as relevant. All things being considered, this author has argued for a Biopsychosocial (BPS) model since the early 1980's. See "Treatise on the Neurophilosophy of Consciousness, a BioPsychoSocial Model of Reality." Penguin Books/Trafford, Inc.)

# Arguments

Emotions. Has there been a paradigm revolutionary shift away from Sigmund Freud's classical approach assigning the rational brain the primary role of, -in response to a relevant stimulus-, triggering the appropriate emotional state behavior, responsible for either harmful or beneficial resulting activity in the decision-making process? Do emotions trigger the rational-driven brain strategies to adapt to environmental stimulation? We always thought it was the other way around! It was not until the 1980's that Nobel prize winner Dr. Herbert Simon (1967) was able to successfully establish the role of emotions on predicting judgement criteria and decision-making priorities, as recent Presidential strategies have illustrated. The importance of emotions is intrinsically tied up to survival of the human species in any or their adopted echo systemic environment. Thus, we need to distinguish between 'needs' and 'conveniences' to survive and their respective association with the exclusive, irreversible, 'unconscious', hormonally-controlled reflex response and the inclusive, reversible, 'subconscious', environmentally-controlled convenient response to any effective stimulation. In the exclusive case of the human species one must add yet another dimension, the 'self-conscious' state which ultimately justifies the additional inclusion of theosophy as an influential argument in a Biopsychosocial (BPS) model of reality where the rational and emotional are given equal weight in the decision-making process. This approach is a significant departure from both the 'emotional' driving force historically associated with the libidinous slave of passions and, contrarywise, the 'rational' driving force, which in an adaptive emotional response to anger, is inhibited from an aggressive response in anticipation of either risk or regret and opts for a rational solution instead. Which of the two options is the absolute solution? This author argues for the best of both options as they best fit the evolving, constantly-changing environment and taking into consideration the genetic and epigenetic make-up of the subject. It is well established that the prefrontal cortex is associated with rational cognoscitive activity in response to ontological, perceptual sense-phenomenal and/or epistemological conceptual activity prior to benefiting from preceding memory recorded activity (including emotional experiences) before a behavioral response or inhibition. When the ventromedial prefrontal area of the brain is accidentally or surgically injured, subjects become more prone to emotionally-driven, sub-optimal, riskier choices when in full conscious knowledge of existing rational choices of action. See: https://www.annualreviews.org/doi/full/10.1146/annurev-psych-010213-115043#

Rationality. There exists good experimental evidence in defense of the brain-induced rationality determinant of judgement and choice of action in response to epistemontological stimulation. However, one may ask, how reliable is the absolute truth content of the exclusive historical language narrative of human subjects about their subjective account on measurable and/or observable objects and events constantly evolving? Furthermore, how do the practical considerations on cost and benefits limit the reliability on computer simulations? There seems to be an important difference between the perceptual, ontological, sense-phenomenal and the conceptual, epistemological memory account of previous objects and/or events. The brief comments that follows illustrates why both accounts are incomplete and a hybrid approach incorporating the best of both epistemontological elements is a better strategy.

To rely on a "Seeing is Believing." ignores the existence of possible micro causal agents beyond the sensory resolution capacity of the human narrator of the micro object or events, from subatomic particles to viruses, etc. But, even two or more subjects witnessing the same object or event may have different memories of what happened! When reacting to the physical presence of an object or event the first brain-recorded reaction is to focus of the meaning and/or significance of the stimulus (is it dangerous, attractive, etc.?) to the subject, then to be followed by more specific details such as color, size, etc., in that sequential temporal order, as recorded in the appropriate 'emotional' region of the brain now in control of the decision-making activity that will follow according the survival needs of the human species.

On the other hand, when later-on the same subject is trying to recall the same past object or event, now physically absent, the human brain tries to re-enact the same experience giving now preference to the 'rational' region of the brain now in control of the decision-making process that will follow according to the survival convenience of the same human subject. The brain-recorded event may even show memories of events that never happened! Which narrative should we trust as the absolute truth of what happened? Is the genetic-driven, hormonal-controlled unconscious reflex activity in behalf of individualized species survival more important than the environmentally influenced, genetic/epigenetic driven subconscious response in behalf of human species survival? Because we live in a constantly-changing environment, competing with other subhuman species for the limited resources for survival, human must learn to share, conserve and socially behave inside our vital bio-psycho-social niche. Thus, we need to introduce the self-conscious state as an epistemological/conceptual, human species survival tool which justifies the incorporation of theosophy and mathematical logic to explain the complexities of the epistemontological Biopsychosocial (BPS) model of reality, life and consciousness.

The preceding reinforcement of the BPS Model was inspired by recent direct recording of the brain activity by 128 electrodes while subjects were under controlled perceptual and conceptual stimulation and recording. See: https://medicalxpress.com/news/2019-01-human-brain-memories.html This updates the last version of the Model which will be briefly outlined below.

# INTRODUCTION

## "A BioPsychoSocial (BPS) Model of Reality, an Update."

The quest for finding the all-encompassing, final theory of everything in reality (TOE) continues un-abated. The front runners' current effort seems to be resting on the premise that the final TOE must exclusively be a "..coherent theoretical framework of physics..." linking all aspects of the universe we all witness. Consequently, models of general relativity and quantum field theories lead the pack by successfully having both been modified because they are mutually incompatible, under a "Grand Unified Theory" to include all dimensions, from the unreachable cosmic infinities of general relativity to the invisible subatomic manifolds of quantum field theories.

This way it includes both, from particles of unit mass to distances of cosmological dimensions. The interactions between these particles unified both leading approaches. when it considered three non-gravitational forces, the "weak", "strong" and "electromagnetic" influences. What seems to be missing from this materialistic physicalist model?

At first sight, the "Grand Unified Theory" seems to deny or ignore the constant change all human observers experience in objects and/or events as a function of time passed. In so doing this physical model naively believes their TOE model will become a truthful 'destination' instead of the necessarily incomplete 'journey' through time where environmental and other relevant changing circumstances continually evolve. What is most amazing is ignoring the inconceivable, fundamental need for maintenance of life and a nervous system which must be part and parcel of any 'Theory of Everything'. Rationality analysis is not superior to the emotionality equivalent of feelings because the latter is admittedly far more complex when ontologically describing and/or epistemologically explaining ever changing objects or events, even with the assistance of mathematical logic. The outstanding feature of gravity in the General Relativity Model, absent from the Quantum Field Theory has triggered a recent interest in 'quantum gravity', 'Membrane' and 'String Theory' and 'dark matter'.

Nevertheless, there cannot be a complete model that can possibly exclude the human narrator of any model. Life must be included, its regulation, biology, etc. The conscious configuration of the physical world is inextricably correlated to the Platonic world, as Roger Penrose suggested. Any narrated account of living, existential reality inevitably becomes a metaphor in poem or prose.

In summary, a biopsychosocial approach, including both the macro general relativity and the micro quantum fields physical model, makes it more complete and as such, better describes how to become better human beings with an improved knowledge of our needs and that of others sharing our ecological niche. It is also true that the current formulation of general relativity and quantum fields represent dimensional extremes of our experience of reality and required re-unification, but it is also incomplete in that it pays no attention to the undeniable influential role played by the observer-narrator/recorder of observed or measured events. A balanced view should include all biopsychosocial features, the biological nervous system, a 'sine-qua-non' condition to have a self-conscious psychological mind individualized and collective social activity to guaranty the survival of the human species. No brain, no self-conscious effort to reunite the required biopsychosocial and theosophical elements.

# METAPHYSICS

---

The BioPsychoSocial (BPS) approach to remedy the incompleteness of the physicalist/materialistic models of reality started in the early 1980 with our publication of "Bocetos para una Biopsicosociología." ISBN 968-18-1867-9 Editorial Limusa, Mexico, Distrito Federal. It has suffered various revisions to update the physical and technological substrates of the biopsychological aspects of brain function related to the theosophy of collective social conviviality. The BPS model has been detailed on "Treatise on the Neurophilosophy of Consciousness." ISBN 978-1-4669-4900-3 Penguin Books/Trafford Publishing, Inc. What follows represents a continuing effort to gather all the relevant "epistemontological" aspects of life and consciousness, including theosophy, to approximate our BPS model to a reliable theory of everything goal.

The higher order BPS consciousness theory aspirations is to eventually become an evolving, yet updated theory of everything (TOE) dynamically incorporating all aspects of human experience, as exposed early on in Wikipedia as follows:

"The 'bps' model of 'consciousness' is a high order consciousness theory in which an unconscious, non-inferential phenomenal state (established from either online sensory receptor input or offline memory input), when confronting a novel life-threatening event, triggers an initially unconscious access intermediate stage where relevant modular networks are incorporated including Broca's language processor recursively co-generating in the process the 'inner language' narrative state and accompanying thought, a conscious high order mental state, all of which causally precedes (or is simultaneous with) the adaptive response (if any, as we see in dreams).

Notice that bps considers phenomenal states to be non-conscious, this would confuse the ordinary reader who expects the Kantian term "phenomenal" to be equivalent to the term "conscious experience". Only the higher order mental state is regarded as "conscious".

The 'bps' model basically describes two co-existing, ongoing mental states, one non-inferential subconscious 'gut feeling' inner sense (BOP, a variant of Lycan's 1996 HOP) and an initially non-inferential unconscious accessing of narrative pathways leading to (recursive co-generation of 'inner language' and thought is an open option) the eventual production of higher order thought (HOT) whose content is the feeling that oneself is the subject of self-consciousness.

In other words, according to the 'bps' theory, feelings are not part of consciousness until higher order thought occurs, i.e., qualia need a context.

In 'bps' theory not even self-consciousness, of which 'qualia' may arguably be considered a subset of, has revealed all of its constitutive secrets. This means that bps is a theory of brain processing rather than a theory of the content of consciousness (qualia) or consciousness itself except when it ventures into the postulate that language and self-consciousness are recursively co-generated or co-causal. More controversial is the mediation of the amygdaloid complex (plo) in providing inherited primitive 'meanings' (proto-semantic codelet) to initiate Chomskyan language processing and thought co-generation, i.e., proto-semantics precedes syntax structuring. For a more complete exposition see:

Further Reading: http://delaSierra-Sheffer.net For a quantum field perspective see also: http://www. biopsychosociology.org http://spaces.msn.com/angelldls /

# METAPHYSICS

Unfortunately, the extraordinary advances in Artificial Intelligence technology has so refined physics, technology and mathematical logic that we have forgotten the fundamental role of human beings, with all its known, inevitable cognoscitive limitations, in this effort. What is interesting is that the materialist/physicalists would not accept that an intelligent design of life can be exclusively demonstrated -with the known laws of physics and mathematical logic- by no other than such limited human being who cannot avoid making decisions outside a belief mental framework! Even Aristotle rested his case beyond the inductive method of the sciences with his defense of an invisible God as the first cause. After all why invest exclusively on the ontological induction when there is so much hidden inside the deductive and theosophy bag of surprises.? Why not ask idealists such as Hume, Kant, Hegel who emphasized more on the linguistic narratives of the epistemological content of self-conscious perceptual ontologies. It must be easy to forget that all epistemological systems evolve from initial descriptive axioms about an existential reality of sensory phenomenal perceptions as measured or observed. Is there an absolute truth with such unstable and changing axioms? Are they mathematically elegant and impressive? No doubt, but are they complete? Ask Godel about their intrinsic limitations!

There have been more recent attempts by Prof. Damasio and others, to expand on the details of what we considered a multilayered, multidisciplinary conceptualization of consciousness by assigning a hierarchy of neurological stages before an internal or environmental stimulus reaches self-conscious level and an adaptive sequential response which Prof. Damasio called an unconscious, primitive unconscious 'proto self', a subconscious 'Core Consciousness' before a self-conscious 'Extended Consciousness.' comes into being. See his year 2000 book: "The Feeling of What Happens."

where a synthesis of sense phenomenal ontological qualia and/or the mind's epistemological activity becomes the effective trigger of an effective, adaptive decisive-action. It should be obvious the tremendous influence memory networks (brains's mental images) and language will have in structuring effective decision-making processes arising out of primitive genetic and/or environmental origins.

# Universal Holism and Individualized Reductionism

**I**

---

What is the difference, if any, between my individualized personal experience and those of the social group I identify with? Is the experience of the group the reliable sum-total of the individual participants' experiences? Likewise, one may ask if the experience of Homo Sapience, wherever in the universe recorded, predictable with reliable certainty> Experience is an account of what happened in the past and is happening now. At the personal level it is conditioned to my sensory-phenomenal perceptual experience as influenced by inheritance and environmentally acquired circumstances in my biosphere. At the group level, experience is best characterized as a shared, common, consensual reality. It is then accurate to consider universal holism as the sum total of the individualized reductions of the whole, and vice-versa?

It becomes immediately clear that the ontological, sense phenomenal, perceptual experience is just a description of any object or event within the resolution capacity of our sensory detectors. Any invisible object or event below such personal or instrumental description can still epistemologically, conceptually explained as a reliable experience, usually under a given set of time/ space conditions. If not, how else can we then talk about invisible viruses, molecules, etc. as participating in a visible disease condition?

By using mathematical logic tools of analysis, we can now predict reliable outcomes in certain interactions between the known and the unknown, between the ontologically visible perception and the epistemologically invisible conceptualization. We are now in a better cognoscitive perspective to proceed with a more detailed structural/functional dissection of our reality, life and self-consciousness before we need to introduce theosophical criteria to compensate for our human species perceptual and conceptual cognoscitive limitations. This way, the conundrum of a biopsychosocial (BPS) model of reality, life and self-consciousness will become clear as it may apply to the various personality types we suffer or enjoy during ordinary, consuetudinary social events as the one considered below for illustration purposes. But first we may ask ourselves, what is it we'd like to converse about, when or where it happened or why it happened to him/her specifically or to anyone, anywhere, wherever in space-time? What degree of completeness or sophistication are we socially aiming at?

**II**

---

'What' refers to the measurable/observed sense-phenomenal, perceptual domain of discourse 'when' linguistically described by a narrator at a given time in space, 'where' it happened under a given set of prevailing conditions (e.g., Standard Temperature and Pressure or STP) until the incompleteness of ontological description makes us to intuitively reach out for an additional, albeit tentative, epistemological conceptual domain explanation about 'why' it happened by using the tools of probable mathematical logic and /or theology.

Some experts (behaviorists, materialists, etc.) prefer the exclusivity of the perceptual/ontological critical analysis while others (philosophers, mathematical theorists, theologians, etc.) prefer the exclusivity of the conceptual/

epistemological model of reality, as e.g., is found in Kantian philosophy where the absolute truth about existential reality lies beyond the limits of all possible human experiences and knowledge, the 'transcendental' approach.

For Kant, the 'transcendental' approach or 'epistemological' domain was a conceptualized empirical argument of a high causal probability value and ontological pretensions where its structural elements were anchored in both measurements/observations of phenomenological objects and events and/or validated conjectures about their probable statistical existence. Such modified comprehensive, multidisciplinary accounts of an evolving existential reality we prefer to label as an 'epistemontological' unit of a hybrid 'biopsychosocial' (BPS) model of existential reality. Consequently, it becomes perhaps unnecessary to invoke a God metaphor to explain the probability of a predetermined harmony as Leibniz -along Plato's reasoning- found necessary in his writings, what we now call 'God' in all the theosophist doctrines.

A 'biopsychosocial entity' understanding includes an analysis of the why, for humans anywhere, it may be true that an object or an occurrence/event may be judged as being evil, harmful, specific or universal, if it only exists in the eyes of the beholder when subjected to an 'individualized' reductionism'. The analysis is now ready to briefly consider some genetic/environmental motivational or intentional forces influencing the reliability of our judgements.

## III

Sometimes we choose to be pragmatic and intentionally try to emphasize on reliable results derived from measurements and/or observations. But, in this case, their meaning is driven by my intention or motive when critically analyzing the results.

Suppose we may wish to evaluate objects or events as to their general potential to either do harm or good, now or in a foreseable future, not personal but transcending the immediate present.

What we are about to narrate is about individuals who represent the whole spectrum of human personality types, from the introvert –> extrovert shy loner –>, etc.

To understand personality types you need to analyze their biological, psychological and sociological (BPS) structural and/or functional component elements and how they amalgamate to become a unit BPS driving personality force.

The biological moiety can be conveniently dissected out to reveal the genetically determined, environmentally steered and socially executed parts. The unconscious neuro-hormone driven features are controlled in their expression by circumstantial environmental operations at crucial times during fetal maturation and early development in the biosphere. This joint interaction of genetic and environmental determinants in any human individual is termed the subconscious. However, when the species survival, as driven by neuro-philosophical considerations of species predatory competition and evolutionary adaptation to a changing environment, is critically examined, we call it self-consciousness. Notice that this is like peeling the surface (self conscious) layer of an onion to see the undersurface (subconscious) layers and subsequent (unconscious) hidden layers until the core sustaining the layers is analytically revealed to simulated vision, taste and smell perceptual equivalents.

But, what if an important feature exists beyond ontological, sense-phenomenal recognition? We then have no choice but to rely on the ontological descriptive consequences of generating Artificial Intelligence (AI) equivalent activity of simulated invisible objects or events. If the measurement values are consistent to all observers, all of the time, under a defined set of space, time circumstances, these epistemological explanations becomes part and parcel of the ontological description.

# IV

Welcome to the epistemontological nature of the biopsychosocial (BPS) hybrid reality as narrated in an adopted language by cognitively limited human beings. So much for the reliability, certainty and absolute existence of objects and occurrences. That is the justification for mathematical logic probability as a necessary and convenient tool to statistically assist in any description and/or explanation of existential reality. Yet, we have no choice but to consider the analytical tools available to use, especially when extrapolating from results obtained from other species, since no other socially advanced pre-human species left narrative linguistic evidence to critically analyze our fast-changing evolving reality. Both pre-human social Bonobos and humans have developed brains and there is good experimental chromosomal evidence linking both species, i.e., all pre-human monkeys have 24 chromosomes resulting from the fusion of 2 chromosomes into the single human chromosome #2 and thus only 23 chromosomes are to be found in humans. Why then only humans were able to leave readable literary evidence of their journey through time?

The human species is the only one demonstrated to be capable of introspectively become aware that s(he) is different from the surrounding environmental biosphere and capable to improve on an inherited primitive Chomsky proto-language to describe /explain his existential reality subsequently. It made possible to distinguish between emotional and rational mindsets controlling Psychosocial behavior both corresponding to their respective primitive, hormonal and evolved rational language.

Do we have emotional or rational personalities? Do we indulge into the delusional grandeur of utopia or surrender to the uncontrollable forces of mental dystopias? Are we free to choose between the two contrasting personality alternatives? At this point we need to further distinguish between a species needs and conveniences. Needs are related to species survival, preferably in good health, happy and socially convivial in harmony with the group he shares the biosphere with., e.g., BPS equilibrium. It exists at all 3 levels of consciousness. Conveniences are exercised by and large, at the self-conscious level of behavior in pursuit of happiness.

If our own cognitive-limited human species, where behavior is determined by inheritance and environmentally acquired influences, are we free? Are we different from other advanced social primates? Another relevant question comes up when we compare the life cycles of humans and primates at the cognitive level. Humans naturally display an adaptive array of complex solutions to a constantly changing environment and share that information with succeeding generations to benefit from. But evolving complexity is not a spontaneous natural event in our biosphere, because things naturally decay as a function of time! Is there an un-natural way or a compensatory activity to make up for our obvious disadvantage in reproductive activity when compared to other species? Why are us humans different?

It is not surprising to explain why any phenomena defying nature's entropy conservation laws of physics is likely the result of an 'intelligent design' by an unnatural entity we all call 'God;. This 'modus operandi' is not different from the conceptual epistemological explanations invoked when dealing with invisible objects or events beyond perceptual ontological description.

# VI

Enter the theosophical domain to assist the cognitive-limited human species with an additional epistemological reasoning tool. Why choose the human species? The evolutionary survival of the fittest in a rapidly changing environment dogma explains it well. In a biopsychosocial environment any theological gathering promoting friendship, cooperation and good will, will do. Arguably, it can be considered not just a 'convenience', but a human dire survival 'needs' sub-serving the preservation of dear life for the species! After all, the circumstantial shadow inevitably always follows the object casting it! Like famous Spanish philosopher Miguel de Unamuno argued, existential life refers to man plus his inseparable circumstance.

But life is a dynamic journey through an ever-changing space time with no certain destination within cognitive reach of the limited human mind to anticipate. It would be interesting to see how the different subsets of consciousness portions out the emotional and rational components of reality to provide a BPS equilibrium. Debary Lodge 8063 in Central Florida became the laboratory observatory where the BPS model theory of the 1980's became alive again. There will never be a more friendly, cooperative, good will club where members, family, close friends and neighbors shared the consequences of their only formal bond, military service, and made life for all so safe and convivial in a complex dynamic social interaction on Fridays (see brief illustration below) and the rest of every week.

# VII

---

At Debary, Central Florida, Veteran of Foreign Wars (VFW) member David was not crazy, but for him any epithet was good enough to bring smiling looks in your direction while you loudly squeak your size 12 tennis shoes against the shiny, waxy terrazzo floor until the latter screams a funny flatulence-like noise. Meanwhile his energetic, attractive wife runs back and forth along the long hall distributing to each guest a copy of some future activity of the 8063 VFW Lodge or the Post Auxiliary Group. Behind her, slowly-walking Sandy, the quietly active, good-looking Club accountant and President of the Post Auxiliary Group, was selling 50-50 tickets to fund and promote the various welfare projects in behalf of disabled veterans or Boy Scouts in any moment of need. Ceiling lights are now dimming.

It's almost 7 pm and the ceiling lights are about to go off except for the beautiful multicolored displays that adorned the ceiling tiles. The busy kitchen, under the efficient control of the entrepreneurial, charming Chef Yolanda and her voluntary 'employees' were busy closing for the night. The musical group rehearsed its drums near an improvised podium arrangement not far from the kitchen area. The dancing was about to start. The kitchen staff soon disappeared through the kitchen back door. Busy waitress Barbara undid her apron and returned to the main Bar counter's high bench seat where her introverted husband was patiently waiting for her. The show was on!

After some brief welcoming remarks to the huge Friday crowd, the Post Commander wasted no time in displaying his unique Saloon dancing 'savoiez-faire' techniques with his elegantly dressed wife, all despite the very limited space available for the dancers to move laterally. The oscillatory wiping movements of the older dancers as they walked was a prominent non-intentional attention seeker.

The place was jam-packed celebrating the 20th anniversary of the original Brooklyn, N.Y. band -Monterrey Jacks-, that now wouldn't leave the Central Florida podiums. Meanwhile the two parallel bar counters couldn't keep up with the brisk business typical of every Friday night. As usual, the Canteen Manager, had taken careful care of all administrative and related non-administrative details since her time of arrival on early afternoon with her inseparable friendly, ailing Marine veteran husband. The distant far end of the wisely decorated hall ceilings was simultaneously hosting a private community party. A riding wall panel, halfway opened, separated both activities while birthday cake from the private party and free salad crossed ways as they moved in opposite directions. Nobody complained and there was always order and smiling looks, an organized friendly little chaos.

# VIII

As usual, some of the un-authorized, non-Member, afternoon and early evening crowds, disappeared after repeating 3 or more times the delicious, crispy whiting fried fish carefully prepared by Chef Yolanda, the only Mardi Gras southern-style chef this side of Central Florida.

Soon after part of the neighbor crowd left through the North side entrance door, another wave of door ringing, card carrying, authorized Members rushed through the front West door. while yet, another neighbor non-member group rushed in through the North side door. Meanwhile some bartenders sitting outside the North side door watched from their smoke-filled tables outside. At the same time the orchestra director had been busy arranging the podium and instruments by the now closing kitchen area, and not at the elegantly decorated far end podium, where the orchestra's ego would have preferred. Several smartly placed round tables had been reserved for the special insider group elite soon to arrive.

Today Friday, at a time when most employed personnel in town are out of work, ready for a relaxation moment at the club before going home, the arrangement of seats was different from Wednesdays, another very popular Karaoke Day. Today's psychosocial expectations of activity would be accordingly display very different, qualitatively and quantitatively.

Just like any other social club, the 'insiders' group had 3 modalities, depending on the psychosocial orientation of the Post Commander and/or his staff, their dissenters and those who couldn't care less, one way or the other.

Under the new administration the club had slowly evolved from the very exclusive Members-only club of the 1980's to become a very popular Members and Debary's middle-class neighborhood 'club'. Members and the mostly upper middle-class non-members from Debary neighborhood established a very friendly functional relationship.

The moment you pulled out and insert your Member card and open the front West door entrance, the orange, western setting sun brightly illuminated the semi dark general area now occupied by the drink toasting extroverts surrounding the main bar counter area on the left. On the right hand side was the immediate entrance to the main bathroom. A few more steps ahead were a set of high table bench seats against the wall where the administrative elite share drinks, experiences and an occasional Friday night free pool table match on their right side. From that wall vantage point they could watch the only other of the three high tables arrangement against a wall, two on their left-near the front entrance- and remaining one directly in front of them -near the side entrance.

If you wanted to know the breaking news on the club's operation, just stand in line at the bar and then listen carefully while you wait for a smiling Sandra or Jodie to serve your special drink concoction which they have already memorized. In stark contrast was the lonely presence of Larry II, patiently waiting for his busy partner, now working at the kitchen's closing routine. Most of the introvert types of personality clients are scattered around, all they needed was an isolated corner or an occasional half empty table. As the evening matured there were a few quasi extroverts-converts as liquor sale lines got larger… and they became more socially conscious. Unfortunately, a few could become aggressive but fortunately not yet in this Debary Post., thanks to the special previous biopsychosocial training orientation peculiar to the military mission to live, let live and survive anywhere, regardless of their heterogeneous composition as driver, nurse, engineer, pilot, physician, lawyer, academic or otherwise.

It was always interesting to watch how two amiable extroverts, retired Post Office guys, used to meet so many people and pets during their many walking mailbox distributions, would socialize with their wives, one would gravitate towards the gambling machines leaving his attractive wife to socialize alone with others. The other one, in contrast, wouldn't take his eyes away from his equally attractive blue-eyed blonde for a moment. In both cases the female looked happy and enjoying the party with their husbands and went home together smiling! Some others wouldn't stop talking to anyone displaying the least interest in the subject matter until they hit a mutually interesting topic. Others would insist in answering their own somewhat related question when invited to react to a very different question by his /her friend at the table. Yet others, with a smiling face, would rather remain silent as they politely listen to one or more simultaneously ongoing dissertations! Some may agree with an original exposition while accepting a contrasting explanation! Finally, another participant may care less about the issue under discussion, one way or the other, regardless of the content because they rather drink and toast for a better material life.

# IX

The one participant enjoying the most profit from his/her physical presence at the Club was the 'non-political' Mayor who doesn't need to identify his party affiliation to promote and defend his political point of view in the most affable, self-indulgent demeanor. This will obviously contrast with introverts who, while having a party affiliation, will prefer a neutral academic perspective when analyzing a psychosocial issue. Others, nonetheless, will tolerate them, offer a drink and pay no serious attention t. C'est la vie when you are de facto socially isolated.

The interesting part of this preceding brief illustration is the analogical diversity between a social Friday evening at the 8063 Debary VFW post in Central Florida and the rest of Continental United States and its territories when the Constitutional democracy features are duly respected and observed while both examples constantly evolve into better places to make friends, cooperate, share, learn in convivial happiness and inspired in good will.

May God bless the Club, its administrators, Members, their families, friends and neighbors and God bless America.

Respectfully, Dr. Angell O. de -la-Sierra, Esq. Life Member VFW. WWW.delasierra-sheffer.net/home.html/

Printed in the United States
By Bookmasters